Book 21—Jesus

Following
the Messiah

Written by Anne de Graaf

Illustrated by José Pérez Montero

Family
Time
Bible Stories

Standard Publishing

Jesus – Following the Messiah

Matthew 8—14; Luke 7—9, 11—13; Mark 3—6

About Jesus—Following the Messiah

The Jews have been waiting for a messiah for many hundreds of years. *Messiah* means "savior" or "rescuer." Some Jews thought the Messiah would save them from conquering nations like the Romans. But those who knew the writings of the prophets knew God's Messiah would come to save His people from themselves.

Jesus is the Messiah for anyone who becomes His follower. What does it mean to follow Jesus? It means choosing to believe in Jesus and all that He promises. It means believing He forgives us whenever we say we are sorry. It means making Jesus our very best friend in the whole world.

When this happens, we enter the kingdom of God. While Jesus is on earth, one of the ways He helps people understand the kingdom of God is by telling them stories. Of those who hear Him, there are many who think His words are just empty tales. This includes most of the Jewish Pharisees, or religious leaders. Between the lines, though, there is always something more that points the people in God's direction. If they want to, they can go that way and learn what it means to follow Jesus, the Messiah. But the choice is theirs.

THE ONES WHO CARED

Jesus and John the Baptist

Matthew 11:2-19; Luke 7:18-35

John the Baptist was in prison. He had told King Herod that living with his brother's wife was wrong, and that made Herod angry.

While John was in prison, he sent two of his followers to Jesus with a question.

"Are You the one who was to come or do we wait for someone else?"

Jesus told them to tell John about all the miracles they had seen Him do. There could be no doubt He was the Messiah.

Then Jesus spoke to the crowd about John. "He is the prophet who made people ready for me. Because you listened to John, you were ready to listen to me."

Jesus said John was the greatest man ever to live. "But even the least important man, if he follows what I have taught, is greater than John."

All the people who had been baptized by John nodded their heads. Yes, because of what John had told them, they had been better able to understand Jesus.

But the Pharisees, who were leaders of the Jews and had not been baptized by John, did not like what Jesus said. They complained and whispered behind Jesus' back.

The Pharisees thought they were very smart. But Jesus told them their kind of wisdom, which was not open to the love of God, was worth less.

She Dared to Say Thank-You

Luke 7:36-50

A Pharisee named Simon invited Jesus for dinner one night. While Jesus was eating, a woman who had lived a sinful life came into the house. She came up behind Jesus and knelt down.

The woman was crying. Her tears ran over her face and onto Jesus' feet. She wiped His feet dry with her hair, and then poured perfume over them.

Simon, the Pharisee, thought to himself, "If Jesus were really a man of God, He would know what a sinful woman this is, and He would not let her touch Him." Simon became more and more upset. But Jesus knew what he was thinking. He looked up and told Simon He wanted to tell him a story.

"There once were two men. One owed a great deal of money to the moneylender. The other owed a little bit of money. When neither could pay back what they owed, the moneylender forgave them both. Now which of them will love him more?"

Simon said, "I suppose the one who owed him the most."

"That's right," Jesus said. "Now look at this woman. When I came into your house, you did not give me any water so I could clean My feet. But she made them wet with her tears and wiped them with her hair.

"You gave me no kiss of greeting, but she has kissed my feet constantly. Do you see? Her sins, which are many, have been forgiven because she loved much. But he who is forgiven little, loves little."

Then Jesus looked down at the woman's tear-stained face. He said, "Your sins are forgiven. Your faith has saved you."

And the guests who were listening wondered, "Who is this man who even forgives sins?"

THE ENEMIES OF JESUS
Whose Side Is Jesus On?

Matthew 12:22-37; Mark 3:22-30; Luke11:14-15, 17-23

As Jesus became more and more popular with the people, it became harder and harder for His enemies to ignore Him.

After Jesus healed a demon-posessed man who could not see or talk, the people asked themselves, "Is this the Son of David, the Messiah, the one we have waited so long for?"

But the Pharisees said, "Look how He orders the unclean spirits to leave people. He must be a servant of Satan, God's enemy, or else the unclean spirits would not listen to Him."

Jesus knew what they were thinking. He told them, "Any kingdom fighting against itself cannot last. If I were for Satan, every time I cast out unclean spirits I would be working against the very one I should be helping.

"But if I cast out demons by the Spirit of God, then God's kingdom is already here," Jesus told them. He said the only one stronger than Satan is God himself. It was by the power of His Spirit that Jesus was able to heal.

But that was something the Pharisees refused to believe.

Woe to the Pharisees

Luke 11:37-42

Through the years the Pharisees had added many rules to the laws God gave

to Moses. There were thousands of rules that only made life more difficult and did not at all help the people to learn about God's love.

One Pharisee asked Jesus to come to his house and eat with him. Even though Jesus knew the Pharisees were His enemies, He agreed. When Jesus did not wash His hands before eating, He broke one of the Pharisees' rules and the Pharisee was surprised.

Jesus told him that clean hands are not as important as clean hearts. "Woe to you Pharisees, because you are clean on the outside, but in your hearts you are greedy and wicked!"

He told them they were like unmarked graves that people walked on without knowing it. They did not show the people the way to life with God.

And Jesus told the teachers of the law,"Woe to you! You and your fathers are the ones who would not listen to God's prophets. You are too proud to do what is right in God's eyes."

After this the Pharisees and teachers of the law were very angry at Jesus. "We must find a way to get Him into trouble," they whispered to each other.

"We will ask Him hard questions and wait for Him to say something wrong," they all agreed.

THE STORIES OF JESUS

The Rich Farmer Who Was Still Poor

Luke 12:16-20

Once while Jesus was teaching, a man said, "Tell my brother to give me some of the money our father left when he died." But Jesus told him, "Don't be greedy. There is much more to life than what you own." Then Jesus told this story.

"There once was a rich man who had a very good farm. The harvest of his crops was so large, this man asked himself, 'What shall I do, since I have no place to store my crops?'

"The man decided to tear down his barns and build bigger barns. 'I can tell myself not to worry,' he said, 'because I have enough things to last a long time. I don't need to work, and I can have a party every day!'

"God said to the man, 'You fool! Tonight is the night you will die! What good will all your money do you then?'

"This is how it will be, Jesus said, for anyone who believes money and things are more important than living for God.

9

The Fig Tree
That Bore No Fruit

Luke 13:1-9

Jesus was preaching in Galilee and was teaching the people that it would not be easy to follow Him. Sometimes it would be painful to do the right thing.

At this time the Roman army ruled over Israel, and sometimes the soldiers were very cruel. A group of men from Galilee had been killed by Roman soldiers. Jesus said that those men had not been worse sinners than anyone else.

Their suffering was not a punishment from God. There is no person who has not sinned.

"But I tell you," Jesus said, "unless you are sorry for your sins and try to live better lives, you will end up destroying yourselves." Then He told them another story.

"There once was a man who had a fig tree in his vineyard. When he came to look for fruit on the tree, he could not find any. So the man told his gardener, 'Cut down that tree. It is useless.'

"But the gardener said, 'Give the tree one more chance. Let it stand a year, and I will take extra good care of it. If, by next year, it still does not have fruit, then I will cut it down.'"

Jesus was saying that the people were like the fig tree. They had been given an extra chance to say they were sorry and start living as God wanted them to. But someday, their chances would run out, and then they would wish they had changed when they could.

10

Sowing Seeds

Matthew 13:1-9; Mark 4:1-9; Luke 8:4-8

Another time, Jesus went down to the beach by the Sea of Galilee to teach. The crowd of people listening grew so large that Jesus climbed into a nearby boat and pulled out into the water a little ways. From the boat, He could speak and everyone could hear Him. There He told them another story.

"There once was a man planting grain seeds in his field. Some seeds fell beside the road, and the birds came and ate it up."

"Other seeds fell on rocky ground, where there was not much dirt. Those seeds sprouted up easily enough, but because there was nowhere for their roots to find water, they died as soon as it became hot.

"Some seeds fell among the thistles and the weeds crowded out the young plants. But other seeds fell on good soil. These plants grew strong and tall. They yielded from thirty to a hundred times as much grain as was first planted."

Jesus looked at all the people on the shore. A few nodded. They understood. But many more were shaking their heads, for they did not know what Jesus was talking about. Jesus said, "Those who are listening, listen very well, and try to understand the meaning of this story!"

Sowing Seeds in the Right Places

Matthew 13:10-23; Mark 4:10-20; Luke 8:9-15

When Jesus told the story of sowing seeds, there were many, including His disciples, who did not know why He talked about seeds. As soon as the crowds left, His disciples asked Him why He told so many stories.

Jesus said that the prophet Isaiah had predicted a long time ago that there would be many who heard Jesus but did not really listen. Then He explained the story of sowing seeds to His disciples.

"The seeds are the lessons I teach. Some people hear these lessons, but because they do not pay attention or they choose to ignore what I say, Satan comes and steals away what little truth they did manage to learn. These are like the seeds planted by the roadside."

"The seeds sown in rocky places are the people who hear what I teach with joy, but after a time, whenever life becomes hard, they go back to their old ways. The seeds sown with the thistles are the people who hear the word but don't trust God to take care of them. They worry and want to make more money, so nothing comes from the lessons they learned. They are worthless.

The seeds that are planted on good ground are the people who listen and practice what they have learned from my words. They tell God they are sorry for what they have done and they change how they live. These people will teach many others about following me."

The Difference Between Wheat and Weeds

Matthew 13:24-30, 36-43

Jesus had another story to tell the crowd.

"The kingdom of Heaven is like a man who planted good seed in his field. Then at night his enemy came and planted weeds together with the wheat.

"When the wheat sprang up, the weeds grew as well. The farmer's workers came to him, asking if they should pull up the weeds. 'No,' he said, 'because you might pull up the young wheat too. Wait until it is time for the harvest. Then gather the weeds and we will burn them. After that we can harvest the wheat.' " Later, Jesus' disciples asked Him to explain this story, and He did.

"The one who planted the good seed is the Son of Man." That is Jesus. "The field is the world. The wheat plants are those who follow me, and the weeds are those who choose to chase after the things of Satan, hurting people and being greedy.

"The enemy who planted the weeds

14

with the wheat is God's enemy, Satan. The harvest will happen at the end of time. The workers in the field are angels.

"So at the end of time, angels will gather those people who have followed my teaching, and they will shine like the sun in God's kingdom. But all the others will be punished."

Mustard Seed and Yeast

Matthew 13:31-35; Mark 4:30-34;
Luke 13:18-21

Jesus had still more stories to tell. First, He said that heaven is like a mustard seed, the tiniest of tiny seeds. But once a mustard seed starts sending down roots, it grows and grows until it is a tall mustard tree. And mustard trees are often the biggest trees in the garden, a place where birds like to make their nests.

Jesus used another story to teach the same lesson. "The kingdom of God is like a small bit of yeast that a woman puts into a large amount of flour." The yeast spreads through all the flour and then bread can be baked and eaten.

Both stories showed that small beginnings in the kingdom of God can grow in great ways.

THE KINGDOM OF GOD

Hidden Treasure and Pearls

Matthew 13:44-46

Jesus asked the crowd He was teaching, "What do you do when you hear there is treasure hidden in a certain field?" The people's eyes grew big.

"You buy up that field so you can own the treasure!" one man shouted.

"That's right." Jesus said. "The kingdom of Heaven is like treasure hidden in a field. When a man found it, he hid it again. And then in his joy he went and sold all he had and bought that field."

That man was willing to give up everything, just to own that treasure.

"In other words," Jesus told the people, "the kingdom of heaven is like a man who looks everywhere for the finest pearls. When he found one worth more money than all the rest, he went away and sold everything he had and bought it."

The man who bought the field and the man who bought the precious pearl, both knew when they had found something very special. Jesus taught that when people ask Him into their lives, they discover it is worth everything, just to grow closer to Jesus and please Him. That is what it means to enter the kingdom of Heaven.

The Fishing Net

Matthew 13:47-50

Many of the people who listened to Jesus' teachings were fishermen. So Jesus talked to them in the words they could best understand, fishing language.

He said, "The kingdom of heaven is like a net that was let down into the lake and caught all kinds of fish. When it was full, the fishermen pulled it up on the shore. Then they sat down and sorted out the fish. They put the good fish into baskets and threw the bad fish away.

"This is how it will be at the end of time. Angels will come and separate the wicked from the righteous, those who have accepted God's forgiveness. The wicked will be thrown into the fiery furnace forever."

The fishermen listening to Jesus tell this story would know just what He meant. Many, many times they had thrown away fish that were too small or did not taste good.

JESUS AS A FRIEND

The Calm

Matthew 8:18, 23, 24; Mark 4:35-37;
Luke 8:22, 23

It often happened that Jesus would spend the whole day preaching to the crowds and healing the sick. At the end of one such day, Jesus pointed to a nearby boat and told His disciples to join Him.

He gave orders to cross to the other side. It was their only chance of getting away from the crowds and Jesus felt He needed the rest. He settled down to sleep at the back of the boat.

At first the water was calm. But although the Sea of Galilee was inland, to sail a boat there could sometimes be very much like sailing on the ocean. A short time later, the boat was in a sudden storm that snuck out of the hills and turned the lake into a whirlpool. All at once, Peter and all the disciples felt very afraid.

The Storm

Matthew 8:25; Mark 4:38; Luke 8:24

The wind kept changing direction. Several times men slipped, but they grabbed onto the side of the boat to keep from being swept overboard by the huge waves. The boat tilted madly from one side to the other. The disciples felt desperate and helpless.

Then, as they both thought of the same thing at once, Peter and John looked at each other. "Where is Jesus?" John ran toward the back of the boat and Peter was right behind him. When they saw Him asleep on a cushion, they woke Jesus up.

Peter fell on his knees before Jesus and said, "Teacher! The sea is wild. I myself am a good sailor, but tonight she is in a fury. Tonight we shall surely die."

John said, "We may not see the morning, Lord. We will die!"

Jesus looked from one troubled face to the other, then He stood. He held up His hands and faced the sea. The wind blew hair into His face. His voice boomed, "Be still!"

The Other Side

Matthew 8:26, 27; Mark 4:39-41; Luke 8:25

As soon as Jesus called out, "Quiet!" Be still!" the wind calmed and the waves disappeared. Peter ran to the edge of the deck, looked overboard and saw his reflection mirrored in the dark sea. He ran back to Jesus and fell on his knees in relief.

"Why are you so timid?" Jesus asked. "How is it that you have no faith?" And He turned to walk toward a part of the boat where no one stood.

The disciples moved toward Peter and John. No one dared speak out loud. An erie silence hung over them all.

"Why does He say 'no faith'?" John asked. "Surely after we witnessed today's miracles we have great faith. What didn't we believe?"

"Don't you remember?" Peter replied. "What did Jesus say when we got into the boat?"

John shook his head and Peter answered for him. "He said we were going to the other side."

The disciples looked at each other in amazement. "Yes," they thought. Once again Jesus had been teaching them about what it meant to trust, to have faith. They looked at Jesus standing at the back of the boat and were filled with wonder. Even the wind and the waves obeyed Him!

21

A Man With an Evil Spirit

Matthew 8:28-34; Mark 5:1-20; Luke 8: 26-39

When Jesus and the disciples landed their boat on the opposite shore, a man with an evil spirit living inside him, came to meet them. For a long time he had not worn clothes or lived in a house. He lived among the tombs in nearby hills.

When he saw Jesus, he ran and fell on his knees in front of Him. Jesus said, "Come out of this man, you evil spirit!"

Then the evil spirit shouted through the man, "What do You want with me, Jesus, Son of the Most High God? Don't hurt me!"

But Jesus asked his name. And he replied, "My name is Legion, for there are many of us spirits in this man." The spirits begged Jesus not to harm them.

A herd of pigs grazed nearby and Jesus commanded the spirits to leave the man and go into the pigs. The evil spirits obeyed. And the very instant they entered the pigs, the pigs ran over a cliff and fell down, into the sea.

There were some men who had been tending the pigs, and they hurried back to town. When all the people came to

see what had happened, they saw the man sitting quietly at Jesus' feet, dressed and in his right mind again.

The people grew afraid of the power of Jesus, and begged Him to go back where He had come from.

The man whom Jesus had healed begged to go with Him. But Jesus said, "No, go home and tell how much the Lord has done for you and how He has had mercy on you."

So the man went away and told people in all the surrounding towns.

Just One Touch

Matthew 9:20-22; Mark 5:25-34; Luke 8:43-48

When Jesus arrived back on the other side of the Sea of Galilee, a crowd was still waiting for Him. A certain man came up to Jesus and fell at His feet. "Please, my little girl is dying. Please come and put your hands on her so she will live."

So Jesus went with him, and the crowd followed. It seemed like there were people pressing in on Jesus from all sides.

One woman was there who had been bleeding inside her body for twelve years. She had spent all her money on doctors, but instead of getting better,

she just became more sick.

This woman came up behind Jesus in the crowd and touched His cloak. She thought to herself, "If I can just touch His clothes, I will get better." And it was true! The very minute she touched Jesus, she felt a rush of warmth flow through her body. She knew without a doubt her bleeding had stopped.

Jesus turned around and asked, "Who touched my clothes?"

His disciples answered, "Look at all the people. They are on all sides of You." But Jesus kept looking around to see who had done it. He knew that power had gone out of Him.

The woman came and fell at Jesus' feet. Trembling with fear, she told Him the whole truth.

He said, "Daughter, because you believed I could heal you, you have been healed. Go in peace. You won't suffer anymore."

Dead, Then Alive

Matthew 9:18, 19, 23-26; Mark 5:21-24, 35-43; Luke 8:40-42, 49-56

While Jesus was talking to the woman who had touched His clothes, the man who had asked Jesus to come heal his little girl waited nearby. This man, who was called Jairus, was one of the Jewish leaders. Although there were many Pharisees who did not like Jesus and were afraid of Him, this man was one of the few who believed Jesus was the Son of God.

As Jairus listened to Jesus, some men arrived with bad news. "Your daughter is dead," they told him. "There is no reason to bother the Teacher anymore."

But Jesus had overheard the men. He told Jairus, "Don't be afraid. Just believe."

Then Jesus had Peter, James, John and the child's father follow Him to the house. The rest of the crowd stayed behind. When they arrived, there were people crying and wailing

But Jesus said, "Why are you making so much noise? The child is not dead. She's just sleeping." The people thought He was crazy. Once He had sent them all out of the house, He took Jairus, his wife and the three disciples and went into the room where the child's body lay on the bed.

He took her hand and said, "Little girl, I say to you, get up!" Right away, she stood up and walked around!

Her mother gasped and ran to hold her daughter. Jairus turned to Jesus with tears in his eyes. He was completely astonished.

"Be sure to give her something to eat," Jesus said.

25

The Blind Are Healed

Matthew 9:27-31

Everywhere Jesus went, people who were hurting in mind and body followed Him, asking to be healed. When Jesus left the home of Jairus, two blind men followed Him. "Have mercy on us, Son of David!" they called out.

Jesus went into a friend's house, and the two men followed. There, He turned and asked them, "Do you really think I can make you see again?"

The two men were friends. They had both heard the stories of Jesus healing people, and together they believed He was the Messiah. They had dared to follow Him from place to place, stumbling along the roads, bumping up against people in the thick crowds that always seemed to surround Jesus. Now they were alone with Him and each took a deep breath. "Yes, Lord," they said.

Then Jesus reached out His hands and touched their eyes. He said, "According to your faith it will be done to you."

Suddenly, the men could see! The first face they saw was that of Jesus, smiling at them. Where there had been darkness, now there was light!

The men were so happy they hardly listened to Jesus' warning that they not tell anyone. They went out and told the news to everyone they met.

"But He Is Joseph's Son"

Matthew 13:54-58; Mark 6:1-6

Jesus and His disciples went on to Jesus' hometown of Nazareth. On the Sabbath day, Jesus went to the synagogue with the rest of the Jews and taught them there.

Many were amazed at what they heard Him say. "Where did this man learn so much?" they asked.

"What kind of wisdom does He have that He can even do miracles?

Isn't this the carpenter? Isn't this Mary's son, the brother of James, Joseph, Judas, and Simon? Aren't His sisters here with us?" They thought Jesus should have been more like them since He had grown up in Nazareth, yet He was so different.

Jesus told them that one of the prophets had said, "A prophet is welcome everywhere but in his hometown. Everyone but his relatives will give him honor."

There were a few sick people who came to Jesus while He was in Nazareth. He healed them, but because so many of the others could not believe that the son of Joseph and Mary was the Son of God, Jesus worked few miracles in Nazareth.

Into the World

Matthew 10:24-42; Mark 6:7-13; Luke 9:1-6

As Jesus and His disciples traveled from village to village, the disciples began to learn how to live as He did.

There were twelve disciples who were especially close to Jesus. They would become the apostles after Jesus died. Jesus sent these men out to teach others and heal the sick. There were more villages and towns in Israel than Jesus could go to himself.

He gave them special orders. Preach this message: 'The kingdom of Heaven is near.' Work miracles and heal the sick. Take no money or extra supplies with you."

Jesus taught these disciples that being His follower would not always be easy. There would be some people who hurt them because they believed in Jesus. Satan would always try to hurt them.

"Do not be afraid," Jesus told them. God the Father will watch over you. He will reward you for anything you have to suffer because you believe in me.

Anyone who welcomes you welcomes me," Jesus said.

"And if anyone gives even so much as a cup of cold water to one of you, he will be rewarded."

Where Is John the Baptist?

Matthew 14:1, 2; Mark 6:14-16; Luke 9:7-9

All the while that Jesus was traveling and teaching, John the Baptist had been in prison. King Herod had arrested John because John kept telling him it was wrong to marry his brother's wife, Herodias.

Herodias hated John. She wanted him killed. If it had not been for Herodias, John would still be free.

But although he had sent John to prison, Herod would not kill him. He knew John was a good and holy man. He knew that the people would do whatever John said, and Herod was afraid of the people. And if Herod sometimes did not understand everything John taught, at least he still liked listening to him.

But Herod was eventually tricked by Herodias into having John beheaded. Sometime after that word of Jesus' miracles and teaching reached King Herod. Some of the people said because Jesus and John the Baptist taught similar lessons, Jesus was John the Baptist. Some said he was the prophet Elijah, come back from the dead. Others said Jesus was a prophet like the prophets of long ago.

When Herod heard all the stories, he, too, thought John had come back from the dead. For this reason Herod was interested in all the stories he heard about Jesus. He wanted to know more.

of the hall. Her feet hardly touched the floor. She was more graceful than any dancer they had ever seen.

King Herod sighed with pleasure. "That is the daughter of my wife, Herodias," he told his friends sitting near him. "Nobody can dance like this."

Slowly but surely, the girl made her way over to Herod until she danced right in front of him. With a last twirl and toss of her head, she knelt before Herod.

The king felt even more drunk than he already was when he looked into her eyes. Not thinking clearly, he said, "Ask me for anything you want and I'll give it to you. I swear it. Ask for anything, up to half my kingdom"

The girl ran off to her mother, Herodias, and said, "What shall I ask for?"

Herodias smiled wickedly. "Ask for the head of John the Baptist on a tray."

When the girl returned to the king and told him her request, the king was very upset. "John is a good man, how can I possibly have him killed?" he worried to himself. He looked around and saw all his friends and the important people watching him. They were waiting to see just how powerful he was. Herod felt weak. "Very well," he told a guard. "Bring me John's head on a tray."

The man went and did as Herod had ordered. When he finally brought back John's head, he gave it to the girl and she gave it to her mother.

When John's disciples and friends heard what had happened, they went to the prison and claimed John's body so they could bury it. And when Jesus heard that John was dead, He was very, very sad.

The King Who Was Tricked

Matthew 14:6-12; Mark 6:21-29

This is how Herodias tricked Herod into killing John the Baptist.

King Herod was having a birthday party. He held a great feast and invited all his friends, family, counselors, generals, and other important people who served him. The palace was full of people laughing and drinking and eating.

The king sat on the floor, leaning on some pillows, drinking wine and laughing with his friends. Suddenly, all the people stopped talking. The musicians had started playing a strange and lovely song.

Everyone turned to watch as a beautiful young woman came dancing into the center

Old Testament